HRJC

W9-AMT-842

CREEPY
MAZES

William Potter
Leo Trinidad

WINDMILL
BOOKS

Published in 2019 by Windmill Books,
an Imprint of Rosen Publishing
29 East 21st Street, New York, NY 10010

Copyright © Arcturus Holdings Ltd, 2019

Written by: William Potter
Illustrated by: Leo Trinidad
Designed by: Stefan Holliland with Emma Randall
Edited by: Joe Harris with Julia Adams

Cataloging-in-Publication Data

Names: Potter, William. | Trinidad, Leo, illustrator.
Title: Creepy mazes / William Potter; illustrated by Leo Trinidad.
Description: New York : Windmill Books, 2019. | Series: Ultimate finger trace mazes | Includes glossary and index.
Identifiers: ISBN 9781538390009 (pbk.) | ISBN 9781508197249 (library bound) | ISBN 9781538390016 (6 pack)
Subjects: LCSH: Maze puzzles--Juvenile literature.
Classification: LCC GV1507.M3 T756 2019 | DDC 793.73'8--dc23

Manufactured in the United States of America

CPSIA Compliance Information: Batch BW19WM: For Further Information contact Rosen Publishing, New York, New York at 1-800-237-9932

CONTENTS

HOW TO USE THIS BOOK

This book is full of high-risk mazes, where you have to help the heroes find a safe path to complete their daring missions. Look out! Every page is packed with perils.

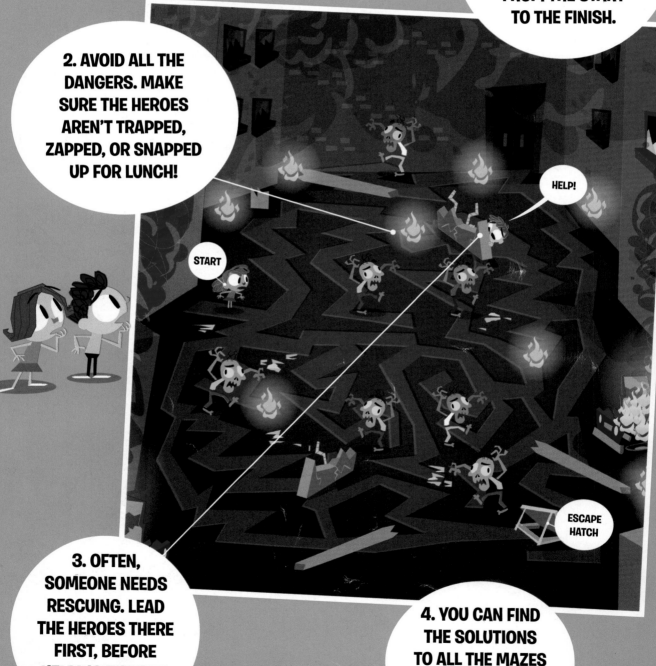

1. READ THE INSTRUCTIONS CAREFULLY BEFORE USING YOUR FINGER TO GUIDE THE HEROES FROM THE START TO THE FINISH.

2. AVOID ALL THE DANGERS. MAKE SURE THE HEROES AREN'T TRAPPED, ZAPPED, OR SNAPPED UP FOR LUNCH!

3. OFTEN, SOMEONE NEEDS RESCUING. LEAD THE HEROES THERE FIRST, BEFORE HELPING THEM TO ESCAPE!

4. YOU CAN FIND THE SOLUTIONS TO ALL THE MAZES FROM PAGES 26 TO 29.

HELP!

START

ESCAPE HATCH

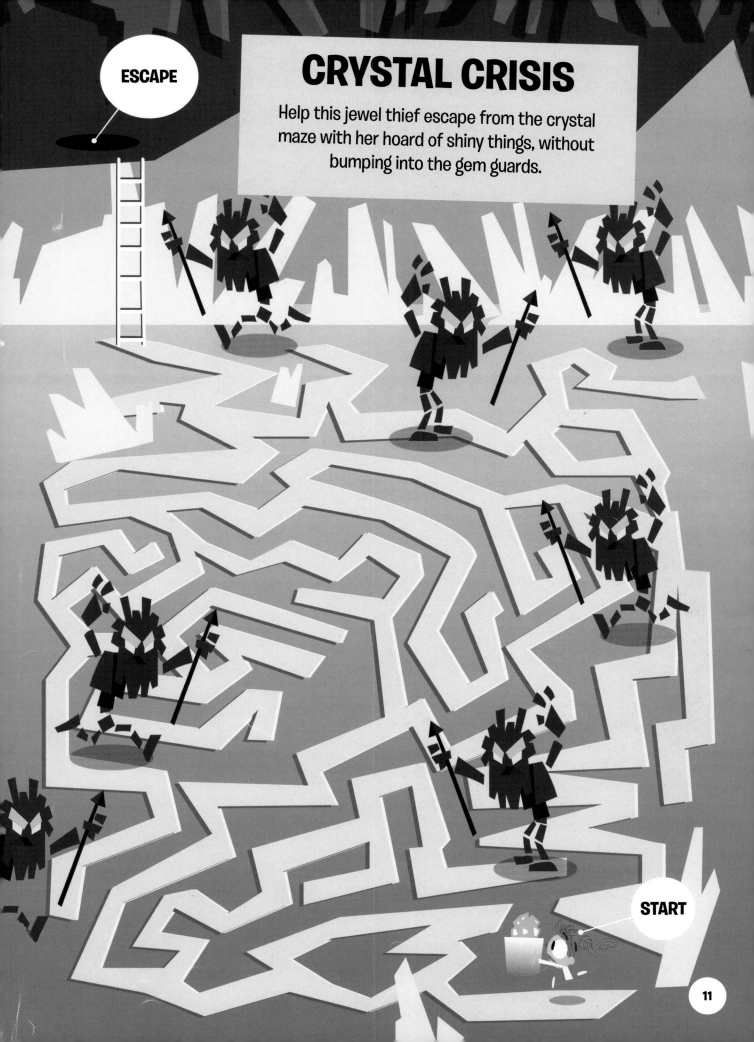

ZOMBIE ZONE

It's the night of the living dead! Dodge the mutant zombies and flames to rescue the boy, then escape underground.

HELP!

START

ESCAPE HATCH

BLOODSUCKING BATS

This boy is in a bell tower where vampire bats are roosting. Help him sneak out without being bitten or ringing the alarm bells!

START HERE!

EXIT

RAMPAGING ROCKS

Save our heroes from being squashed by stone giants. Lead them past the perils to the exit.

BRAVE THE BUGS

The forest is a fright when you're tiny! Can you find the quickest way to the growth ray, before this adventurer becomes a bug's breakfast?

GROWTH RAY

START HERE!

CRAZY CROP CIRCLE

These alien investigators are trapped in a crop circle guarded by cyber-crows. Help them to escape in their limo.

ESCAPE

START!

FRIGHTENING FOG

A thick fog has descended on the old town. Help the kids get home by avoiding the gas clouds and barrels.

HAUNTED HOUSE

These two intrepid ghost hunters need a way to escape the haunted house without meeting any sinister creatures.

18

MEET THE MINOTAUR

Lead the Greek hero through the maze to fight the monstrous minotaur and end his reign of terror.

FACE THE MINOTAUR!

START HERE!

TIGHTROPE THRILLER

High above the canyon, a daring tightrope walker has to reach the other side without bumping into perching vultures.

START HERE!

FINISH

22

SNAPPING STONES

Some of these stepping stones have teeth! Find a way across them, but keep off the biting boulders.

MAXIMUM OVERLOAD!

The power plant is ready to blow. Help the heroes reach the control panel and switch it off before it all goes bang!

SOARING SUPERHERO

Doc Tentacle has taken the mayor! Help the city's superhero follow the heat trail and dodge the claws to save her.

HELP ME!

START HERE!

CREEPY MAZES
SOLUTIONS

PAGE 5

PAGE 6

PAGE 7

PAGE 8

PAGE 9

PAGE 10

PAGE 11

PAGE 12

PAGE 13

PAGE 14

PAGE 15

PAGE 16

PAGE 17

PAGE 18

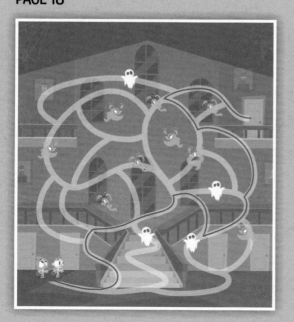

PAGE 19

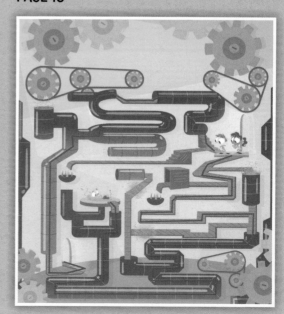

PAGE 20

PAGE 21

PAGE 22

PAGE 23

PAGE 24

PAGE 25

GLOSSARY

crop circle An area in a field of crop that has been flattened into a circle or similar geometrical shape.

crypt An underground room.

descend To move downward.

fortress A reinforced military base or secured town.

intrepid Brave or fearless.

investigator A detective; someone who solves crimes or investigates accidents.

menace A threat or danger.

minotaur A creature from Greek mythology who is half human, half bull.

mutant A creature that is different from its parents due to changes in its genes.

petrifying Very scary.

pharaoh In ancient Egyptian king or queen.

ravenous Extremely hungry.

scarab A beetle that was sacred in ancient Egypt.

snared Caught.

tomb A room, often underground, where dead people are laid to rest.

FURTHER INFORMATION

Books:

Artymowska, Aleksandra. *Around the World in 80 Puzzles*. London, UK: Big Picture Press, 2017.

Kamigaki, Hiro. *Pierre the Maze Detective: The Search for the Stolen Maze Stone*. London, UK: Laurence King Publishing, 2015.

Robson, Kirsteen. *Space Maze Book*. London, UK: Usborne Publishing, 2016.

Smith, Sam. *London Maze Book*. London, UK: Usborne Publishing, 2018.

Websites:

For web resources related to the subject of this book, go to: www.windmillbooks.com/weblinks and select this book's title.

INDEX